I HOPE THIS REACHES HER IN TIME

Also by r.h. Sin

I HOPE THIS REACHES HER IN TIME

r.h. Sin

Andrews McMeel
PUBLISHING®

Andrews McMeel Publishing
a division of Andrews McMeel Universal
1130 Walnut Street, Kansas City, Missouri 64106

www.andrewsmcmeel.com

22 23 24 25 26 RLP 10 9 8 7 6 5 4 3 2 1

ISBN: 978-1-5248-8079-8

Library of Congress Control Number: 2022941950

Editor: Patty Rice
Art Director/Designer: Diane Marsh and Julie Phillips
Production Editor: Lauren Manoy
Production Manager: Shona Burns

ATTENTION: SCHOOLS AND BUSINESSES

Andrews McMeel books are available at quantity discounts with bulk purchase for educational, business, or sales promotional use. For information, please e-mail the Andrews McMeel Publishing Special Sales Department: specialsales@amuniversal.com.

THE AGONY

the joy is replaced
with sadness
your expectations
become disappointment
the truth was just
an attractive lie
a bunch of letters
forming words
that came together
to create sentences
of manipulation
the heart becomes cold
as if to lose its summer
the soul becomes tired
you and your restless spirit
what's behind those dead eyes
you wear that blank expression
like new skin
you wear sadness like the latest fashion
you wear pain like garments
you've been draped in anguish
don't you miss who you were
before who you became
took over your life
do you miss yourself
like I miss you

do you even remember
what it felt like to be happy
have you forgotten yourself
beneath your troubles

and all of this for a love
that turned out to be hatred
all of this for a heart
that never deserved yours
all of this hurt for a relationship
that would never work
all of yourself
all of everything
invested into something
that now feels like nothing

good women are tired of giving
their love to people who do nothing
but break their spirit
mighty women are tired of using
their strength to hold on to relationships
that aren't worthy of their energy
these women are capable
of walking away and they will

_____

You're silent because despite expressing
how it hurts, they still decide to hurt you.

The heart of a person cries more than the eyes.

For once, you'd like to be with someone who feels attached to you as much as you feel connected to them.

Somehow you apologize when they hurt you
because you started believing it's your fault.
It's not.

———————————————

Please don't make me believe that you love me when you never intended to stay in the first place.

the most fucked up thing
about not being sad
is that sometimes
you're still not actually happy

you're somewhere between
the chaos and peace

sure, you want joy
but you're expecting hell
because that's what
you're used to

please don't ignore me
because I make time for you
please don't forget me
because I'm always considerate
please don't replace me
because I'm not searching
for anyone else

thinking about someone all the time
is not enough to make them
deserving of your thoughts

sometimes it's not a sign
it's just something you do
until you don't

sometimes
it's the feeling
of being sad
tired and lonely
that forces you back
into the arms of
the person who
made you sad
tired and lonely

———————————————

the quietest of people
scream the loudest
on the inside of their heart

sometimes you miss having
that person to talk to
but you mustn't forget
that most of the time
they were never really listening

this type of exhaustion
can't be fixed with sleep

you more than likely
will never forget him
but with time
you will find someone
worth thinking about
worth remembering

you texted to say
"I'm okay"
but there were tears
falling from your face

you said it was fine
while falling apart
where no one could see

Fuck him for telling you everything you wanted to hear just so that he could get everything he never deserved.

He says you're beautiful, but how could he
be so ugly toward you? He says he misses
you, but he's the reason you're apart. He
claims to love you, but why do you always
feel like he hates you?

it's hard
wanting someone
to know something
that you don't
want to tell them

———————————

they love you when they're lonely
and that love will never be enough

---

it hurts
but not too much
to hide it

the heartbreak
can make you selfish
you tend to hurt people
before they could ever
get the opportunity
to hurt you

and you expect the pain
to eventually find you
and so you run from anyone
who may be capable
of destroying your heart
like the last person did

caring for someone
means handing them
a knife and hoping
they never cut you
and this is what
scares you the most
because your scars
are symbols
of how often
you've had to survive
being with the wrong person

there are no tomorrows
when you're with the wrong person
it's like the future pushes itself
further away from your grasp

and the love you say you want
dies slowly in the distance
until you give it life
by letting go and moving on

———————————

there was
no more light
in our star
and it took
several nights
to realize this

they'll apologize once they get caught
they'll beg for a second chance
a new opportunity to find new ways
to hide all the things
they'll always do behind your back

his lies held her hostage
she struggled to break free

what's the use of someone who stays
if all they bring with them is hell

I hope you understand that you can't keep fighting for someone who is okay with losing you.

you have spent
too much of your time
wondering whether or not
you are good enough
and not enough time
realizing that the person
you're fighting for
will never be brave enough
to love you back

just because a person wants you
doesn't mean that same person
will do anything to keep you

you tried
you still care
you're done fighting
your heart feels empty

eventually the girl you took for granted
will take her love and give it to herself
and someday someone better than you
will love her in all the ways you couldn't

it's so easy to feel forgotten
somewhere lost behind the noise
gasping for understanding
shouting things
that no one seems to comprehend
constantly screaming
but you're invisible now
still fighting to be heard
at war searching for peace

I could feel myself shrinking beside my
need for you. Somehow the love I'd invested
into our relationship began to outgrow and
overshadow the love I should have
cultivated for myself. And so it shouldn't
come as a surprise that when you left, I felt
so fucking small.

You're with a person so damn long that you believe abandoning the idea of things getting better means losing a future that could improve, and so you just stay there despite the breaking of your own heart, hoping that it'll be worth it in the end. But the truth is, sometimes it's not. I've seen many faces beaten down by time and a belief in hope. I've witnessed many people grow old with the regret of not leaving sooner, and I hope you don't have to suffer that fate.

I know you want to be the one who changes them, but nothing you do will ever be good enough for the person who doesn't deserve your love and energy. I know it hurts, but you can't continue to hold on to someone who stands in your way of finding real love. Life is too short to be in a relationship that distracts you from being happy. Some people are incapable of comprehending their partner's worth, and it is not your job to make them a believer.

Sometimes you're so emotionally drained
that you don't even have the energy to move
on. You stay longer than you should,
wasting whatever you have left, hoping that
somehow things get better.

Sadly, he's not holding on to you out of love. He's sticking around so that you can feel stuck. Some men would rather keep you from finding the right person instead of changing their behavior.

You get hurt so often by fraudulent people, and this is when you finally realize that real is rare.

Sometimes the people who have to lose you to appreciate you don't deserve a second chance.

So often, being told that you're beautiful by
someone who makes you feel ugly inside . . .

Never trust a man who claims to love you
but keeps you hidden.

_____

The fact that you're searching for a sign is a sign that you're unsure, and if you're unsure, you are unhappy, and if you're unhappy, you should leave.

Don't let them make you believe that sex is
the only thing you have to offer . . .

There's a difference between waiting for the one and waiting for the person who keeps hurting you to become the one. Don't waste your time.

don't build your future
on fragile ground

———————————————————

The first time could be a mistake, but the second is a habit. Walk away from anyone who continues to act in ways to hurt you.

Something tells me I'm going to have to lose
you to gain back my peace of mind.

the joy in your heart
was not meant
to be shared with
someone who wants
you to compromise
being happy

I wish I had more energy
to give myself
after wasting
these years on you

It's fucked up when the thing you love the most is a detriment to your happiness.

It's fucked up to want love and yet hold on
to someone who acts like they hate you.

It's fucked up that the fear of being alone has kept you in a relationship with someone who makes you feel alone.

It's fucked up that you find yourself
apologizing for reacting to the way they
treat you.

It's fucked up that your first lessons in love
were taught by someone who didn't actually
love you.

It's fucked up how the people who expect you to trust them automatically are also the people to betray you the most.

It's fucked up that the people you'd do anything for are the ones you often can't depend on.

It's fucked up that you relate to the things written here, and I'm sorry.

─────────────────────────

It's fucked up that in your journey for love
and understanding, you've been met with
heartache and confusion.

I know you're strong, but that doesn't mean
this shit doesn't hurt, and even though you
will get through this, it doesn't make it any
better.

drops of rain on windows
the city looks like you
as melancholy fills the streets
the chill in the air
feels like your breath
and the weather resembles
everything that sits within your soul

you are cold, at times numb
you run from the feeling of it all
sometimes you simply walk
but either way it all catches up to you
like darkness consuming light
and you are once more reminded
of all the things
you force yourself to forget

aren't you tired of this shit
the constant struggle
the feeling of loneliness
while lying next to the one
who promised to love you
but never kept their word

waiting for change, afraid to accept
that it won't get better

aren't you tired of their shit
the back and forth
not knowing where you stand
the wars, all this fighting
without the feeling of victory
all you've felt is defeat

the girl who deserves the sun
is tired of being rained on

the girl you don't appreciate
will get tired of loving you

my generation is filled
with lovers who will never know
the true meaning of love

relationships that feel more
like a prison term
and a happiness
that is simply a delusion

my generation, filled with chaos
no peace, it's difficult, it's complicated
it's nothing, it hurts, it gets worse

you were the emptiness I felt
you were darkness consuming me
you were the thing
keeping me from happiness

I was the ocean
you wanted rivers
I was the moon
you chased the stars

I needed to find myself
but you were
keeping me from me

the years I spent
losing myself
while trying to keep you

1:11 in the morning
my heart is searching
for a feeling that doesn't hurt

my mind just wants
to think of something
that'll make me smile

my heart breaks with yours
my soul, just as restless
as your own

I fall beside you
I understand your silence
and you are not alone

we find time to waste
remembering the faces
we struggle to erase

we give energy to those
who give nothing in return
we learn the hard way
but instead of letting go
we stay

we fall in love with relationships
filled with hate
we become content with giving
ourselves to the wrong mate

crashing into walls
worsening our wounds
deepening the bruises

the endless cycle of recycling
relationships
that no longer deserve
our attention
being attentive to lovers
who pretend to care
constantly showing up
for others who are never there

you are chained to the past
it's time to free yourself

she made oceans
with her tears
she used the heartache
as motivation to build
the boat in hopes of sailing
far away from everything
and everyone who hurt her

the moon is watching you
it hears your sighs
it witnesses your struggles
to close your eyes

she wore loneliness
in a smile
she hid the sadness
with laughter

the clouds dance around each other
like lovers avoiding the truth

all of her stars are burning

cry
empty yourself
of all the pain
he caused you

I was killing me
to give us life
I was drowning
to save the person
who kept pushing my head
under water

someday your soul
will no longer linger
in places where pain exist

I won't judge you
or criticize you
for doing what you've done

I only wish you saw
what I see
when I look at you

I only wish you wished
for more than
what you've settled for

you are not a phase
you are not some trend
you are more than
just something to do
for the moment

more than a hobby
more than you may even know

you are more
and you deserve
more than what
they're willing to give you

there are so many wars
going on at night
so many hearts are fighting
to survive without light

the darkness contains
everything we should forget
the regrets are magnified
the night is plagued with what ifs

you, reading this
your eyes dancing on this page
you, the one who knows
how it feels to have their heart
racing out of their chest
overrun with anxiety
desperate for relief
it is you who wants to be loved
understood for everything
that you are

it is you, the one reading this
the one who is close to tears
so close to breaking
it is you who will save yourself
because this is what
you've always done
because you are strong enough
to do so

dancing to the silence
of the night
we sway like a bed of roses
in the wind

he only loved you in the dark
in secret, behind closed
bedroom doors
he was yours, until he came
and then he left
whenever he was done
draining you of everything
he never deserved

aren't you tired of a love
that feels less than everything
you claimed you wanted
has your soul grown weary
of being with someone
who only wants you for a nut
someone who cums
but never stays

your heart deserves better

I was standing here
the whole time
my heart in my hand
prepared for commitment
and eager to love
but you didn't see me
until after it failed
with the others
and I decided not to be
your second choice
your last-ditch effort at love

I refused to be the one you chose
after the ones you overlooked me for
refused to choose you

I was standing here the whole time
but you decided not to see me

it was raining in the park that day
she was sitting on a bench
mid-may, wearing the eyes of sadness
and for the life of me
I couldn't tell if she was crying
because her tears would have blended in with the rain
her soul as dark as the afternoon sky
and I said nothing
but wondered why
the girl sitting alone
hand clutching her phone
at a loss for words
with so much pain in her heart

he calls but mostly
when he needs something
haven't you noticed
pretending to give a damn
about your day
just to get his way

the manipulation hurts
but you'll sit there
and make excuses for him
seeing what you want
hearing one thing
and thinking another
whatever helps with
the delusional
because the truth
is so much harder
to accept

foolish of me
to believe that

a dysfunctional family
could function in a way
that made me feel loved

just like any and everything else
things are never what they seem
people change or maybe they simply
revert back to everything
they're supposed to be

you mean to tell me
that you're so afraid
of being alone
that you've decided
to hold on to the one person
who makes you feel lonely
even while sitting beside them

you keep saying you want real love
and yet you've chosen to entertain
the same person who will never love you

the heart wants what it wants
and it's too bad that the heart
your heart, doesn't want the one
who deserves you

I'd tell you to let go, but you'll just say
it's easier said than done

typical, predictable
claiming to be in love
with someone who has done nothing
to make you feel loved
someone who
has done nothing
but make you hate yourself
and sometimes
you hate them just the same

I wish your desire
to be happy
somehow outweighed
your tolerance for the heartache
they've caused you

are we still pretending
that it doesn't hurt
holding on to broken relationships
in hopes that someday they'll work

are we still holding on
using the last bit of strength
we have, on lovers who only
wish to use us up then toss us out
like a piece of notebook paper
filled with errors

are we still listening to liars
who say whatever
they need to say
just to get
another opportunity to hurt us

are we hurting yet saying nothing
it's painful but we've kept quiet
in hopes that things will change

are we . . .
are you . . .
am I . . .

your father, the first man you knew
the first man you'd love
one half of the reason why
you grew up so hard

so young and yet
your heart began to ache
breaking into a million pieces
as you alone would learn
to pick yourself up

your father the first man
to disappoint you
the first man to let you down
the first man to cause you
to lower your expectations

he loved you, yes
but I guess not enough
to protect you
as you loved him enough
to look past his failures

you'd go on to accept
his half-ass efforts to love you
you'd go on to accept men
and their half-ass efforts to love you

your father, only present
just enough for you
to feel like you mattered

your lovers only present enough
to fool you into thinking they cared

I used to wonder to myself
how could you ever love a man
who barely made an effort
but then I witnessed your father
as he barely tried
and with tears in your eyes
you said you loved him
your father taught you
how to love men
who reminded you of him

beneath a jacket
two sizes larger
than your body
your arms folded
as if to keep your secret

you hid yourself
from the world
because the world
betrayed you

the robbing of your innocence
an inappropriate touch

behind those walls
behind the barriers
that keep the world
from your heart
is a woman worth
fighting for

behind those walls
that tall, strong
separation from the world
lives a love worth
wishing for
you are greater than
what has happened
you are far greater
than what occurred in your past

behind those walls
behind that cement
that has kept others
from hurting you
like the ones from before
lives a love that only you
can provide, a love like yours
is worth climbing the wall
that sits in front of your heart

what we love should inspire us
who we love should inspire our strength
but you have fallen for hands
not worthy of your skin
you have fallen for a mind
that will never understand your value
you have fallen for a heart
incapable of loving you
the way you need

what we love, what you love
should feel like paradise during the storm
the person you love should feel like stillness
during an earthquake

but you've fallen for someone
who will never be able
to be brave enough to fall for you

the night will fade away
and so will the darkness
the moon will float into the abyss
and the sun will announce itself
with a ray of light and hope
and warmth and beauty
the morning will come
the day will begin
and the corners of my room
the dark corners of my room
will be filled with a light
that will kill off all the things
and all the pain that haunts me
during the rising of the moon

the sun will sit in the sky
and it will shine providing its light
giving me enough time
and a peace of mind to evade you
because you live in the midnights
where I feel hopeless
filled with despair
you live in the night
the darkness,
the restlessness the air
of uncertainty

you live in the moments
where my eyes cannot close
you survive in shattered dreams
and the bruising of my soul
but just like the night you fade
behind the horizon, and just like the sun
I rise, possibly brighter
and stronger than before

the morning will come
the day will begin
and you will be forgotten
once more

miss me like archers with bad aim
lose me like hands on a rope
incapable of holding on
regret leaving me
like the sun does the sky

my absence like a slow death
that you'll struggle to survive
look for me like eyes struggling
through darkness
reach for me like lungs
struggling for air
search for me
like the meaning of words
search for me where you left me
and I will no longer be there

telling her she's beautiful
while destroying
her confidence is abuse

telling her you love her
while acting as if
you hate her is abuse

filling her up with false hope
with no intention of changing
or doing better is abuse

I fell in love with hopes of you remaining
the reason I smile, but you were hell, and I
didn't deserve to get burned.

what was once our home
became a haunted house
and we moved through
each room like ghosts

the broken embodiment
of what we could have become

the dream no longer alive
we replaced our love
with nightmares

you promised not to get lost
but I woke up one morning
unable to find you
behind the lies you told

I wish it were as easy
as telling sadness
to leave me be

but the sorrow
follows me home
and sleeps beside me
during nightfall

It's fucked up because all the energy and effort you've invested into the relationship goes unnoticed. The person you're fighting for is never present enough to comprehend the sacrifices you've made, and even then, deep down, you hold on to this belief that things will somehow get better. You refuse to let go because you feel like you're giving up, and you may have failed to realize that if that person isn't making the same effort, then your fight is all for nothing. And if you're fighting for someone who isn't matching your devotion, you lose nothing when you leave them.

I just want you to know that it gets better, but for things to change, you're going to have to make one of the most challenging decisions you've ever made. You have to let go; you have to allow yourself to find the freedom in being alone rather than with the wrong person. You have to let go and choose yourself for a change. Listen, if you're strong enough to love a person unconditionally, especially when that person refuses to love you back, then you are also strong enough to let them go and live alone until you've found the right person to share in your happiness and peace.

There is a loneliness that lives within the walls of being with the wrong person, and you house yourself in misery the longer you reside there. Though the foundation is always weak, the surrounding structure that boxes you in feels impenetrable, and while you wish to find an exit, doors and windows appear to be obsolete. It's suffocating, really; you struggle for air, for freedom. The opportunity to find peace dissipates the longer you remain there. Your future begins to fade beneath the realization and struggle of putting this particular relationship in the past.

Being with the wrong person is hell. You want love; deep down, you know you deserve it, but you compromise that idea of peace to hold on to a person who fills your head with chaotic thoughts. You want happiness, but the joy is replaced with madness and sorrow. You try your hardest to look past the pain because you want to stay, but you don't even realize that the person in front of you simply distracts you from the life you say you want. It's not going to be easy, but this person you've settled on has made life more complicated, so you will have to find the courage to leave them behind. A better tomorrow never arrives to those who are still entertaining the things that should be left behind, given to the past. Again, I know it's not easy, but you must find your way out. You have to stop devoting your energy to holding on and dedicate yourself to the process of moving forward.

THE TRIUMPH

nothing about you is weak
yes, you may feel broken
you might have felt tired
but it is your strength
that has allowed you to love
it is your strength
that has allowed you
to hold on
and it is your strength
that will grant you permission
to move on from this

it's painful
this isn't easy
but you're a flower
growing through
a drought
and you will bloom
throughout the chaos

you are a whole story
do not paraphrase your chapters
for someone who can't comprehend
the meaning behind the words

she is cinderella
with a fucking axe
not waiting
to be saved
she's ready to fight

you can't be a mansion
to a man who only wants
to occupy motels

at times you feel broken
but those scars are proof
that no one can destroy you

you have mastered the art
of piecing yourself back together
the heartache is transformative
you have found strength and meaning
beneath the rubble, the chaos
and destruction

you have run through storms
so often that you've become one
a force that can't be ignored
with power so profound

you see fire; you're not afraid
you've learned to see
the inspiration in the flames

there's no battle you can't win
there's no mountain you can't climb
you see obstacles; you see the enemy
you see everything that you can conquer

give yourself permission
to forfeit your participation
in any relationship
that doesn't bring you peace

you've heard stories
about the woman
you are now

they almost sound like myths
but you are the proof

war stories and scars
battles fought
in the thick of darkness

a fiery testimony of survival
your story of how
you faced chaos
and transformed it
into glory

look back at what
you endured
whenever you feel
as if you won't make it
because you will
you always do

---

a time to commit to yourself
a moment to heal your wounds
some time alone for clarity
some time on your own
for rediscovery

you are an entire story
do not entertain anyone
who intends only to read half

you learned you could fly
the moment the ground
beneath your feet
began to crumble and sink

you think you're running on empty
but maybe that's not it
perhaps you're being fed
from a source
you haven't found yet
a place you never knew existed
until this very moment

you have always been
everything that is right
about love
and it's okay
that there have been times
where your love
has fallen into
the wrong hands

I'll be honest; it'll sting now and then. Those memories, the things you've tried your hardest to bury, will resurface time and time again. There will be moments where you stand firm despite those chaotic emotions, and there will be days where that same chaos can and will bring you to your knees. And if there's anything I can share with you, a suggestion to consider. Just let that shit hurt, be honest about the way it feels, and eventually, it'll pass, and you'll figure out how to compose yourself.

you could hold the stars
if you up and decided to
the moon would be yours
forever if that's what you wanted

the thunder and lighting
could perform for your
darkened skies
if you set the stage

tonight, my love
just say the words
and it can all be yours
because it's what you deserve

the darkness
that's where you found
your fire, that light, the power

don't be afraid of the nights
that teach you to shine

a man, losing time for you
is a man making time to be
with someone else

the triumph is realizing
that you must leave
even if you're struggling
to do so

you stopped holding on
that's how you held
yourself together

Your words are powerful, and the things you say matter. It's one thing to believe in the difficulty of moving on, but the more you tell yourself that you can't do it, the longer it'll take. I know it's easier said than done, but you must understand that you alone have had to make tough decisions your entire life, and this is just another opportunity to do what's best for yourself. Believe you can, and one day you will.

the beauty of you stretches
far beyond the surface
buried somewhere deep
beneath the bone

proliferating despite the heartache
bursting through skin
and sprouting up toward the heavens
you bloom, my dear

look at how far you've come
to arrive at a presence of peace
you took hell and transformed it
into a lesson on how
to create a version of heaven
for yourself, a place of rest
for weary bones and a tired mind

look at how far you've walked
ran at times, felt stuck often
fighting the urge to go back
pushing your limits
to move forward

and when the sky began to fall
it couldn't keep you
the storms could not hold you
because you carried yourself
toward victory

when you struggle to keep going
just look at how far you've come
to get to where you are now

where there was once a bridge
a wall is being built
and on it, a painted mural
a portrait of you
in remembrance
of the strength it took
to let go of people
who didn't deserve
to reach you

a woman pushing forward
is an artful movement
a celebration of no longer
allowing chaos
to run her life

a woman pushing forward
is a poem based on the strength
and understanding
the realization
that she alone can set
herself free

show me mountains
and I will introduce
you to the woman
capable of moving them

that woman is reading
this right now

you couldn't tell at first
but when you fell
toward that fiery hell
of heartache and confusion
forcing you to believe
in that illusion
the awaking of your delusion
that somehow this pollution
would be the cure, the fix

you couldn't tell at first
but this person
was always full of shit
you see, love is a puzzle
and this individual
could never fit
could never live
in your future
because there are
no benefits

you couldn't see it at first
the disaster, that curse
broken by your desire
for better over worse

you couldn't see
but then you did
letting go
can feel like death
but in moving on
you live

scared, alone
fighting, tired
restless past midnight
struggling to rise
beside the sun

you make pain
look like inspiration
it hurts
but you see the lessons
the blessings in breaking

the song in a storm
a melody derived from rain
the days are dark
the skies are gray

but you are
and will forever be
the proof for what occurs
when a woman decides
that she can't be stopped
and there is nothing
or no one that can stand
in her way of self-love

women are not hobbies

women are not doormats

women are not revolving doors

there's a beautiful riot
in her voice
waiting to be heard
destined to destroy
the chains that kept her silent

I want more than anything for the woman reading these words to feel seen, heard, and understood. I want her to find the fire that has been lost, hidden deep within her heart. The fire that she's been distracted from while loving someone who chose to silence her. What I want more than anything is to witness your greatness, Queen. I want to see you cultivate the love and joy you deserve in the absence of the person who tried to destroy you.

_____

cry, wash him out of your system

you gave an angel hell
and she became a phoenix

she's a quiet wild
gentle sort of rough
something divine
but rarely understood
always to be adored
and respected

_____

he's full of shit, you know

and no, you don't need to be more patient

and no, you don't have to fucking apologize
for wanting more from him

and no, you're not complaining when
demanding what you deserve, especially
when it's what you've given him

no man has the right to make you feel
insignificant, nor should you minimize your
presence to make him love you because a
man who wishes to shrink you and force you
to compromise who you are for his love and
attention will never be worthy of your love
and attention

break the tradition
of making friends
out of exes
who never
respected you

end that toxic cycle
of making room
in your life
for things that don't
deserve to stay

when you look into the mirror
I hope you see more than a reflection
I hope you see home

tethered to a dream of love
you let go of a relationship
filled with nightmares

sometimes
you have to run
through hell
to know where
heaven exists

you are the wildest flower
dancing through summer
reaching toward the sun
naked in the wind
rooted in magic

I hope you find a relationship
that lasts as long
as the moments in our memories

may your rain
remain heavy
your storm
always strong
and your fire
refusing to surrender

you are the rain
when your flower
needs a drink
you are the light
when stuck
in darkness
be unto yourself
everything you need

poetry lives
in the lining
of your skin
you are a masterwork
of strength and love
being told in the most
beautiful of ways

there's so much
peace and quiet
in being single

that alone is a gift

never hold on
to a person
who makes you feel
like you must ask
for permission to be loved

you're not cold
you're just keeping
your warmth
to yourself

refusing to waste
your summers
on the wrong person

the time it took
to hold on
will be the time
it takes to let go

be patient
with yourself

I look toward the night sky
to see more stars than usual
and I think to myself
that at your request
these stars are serenading you
during midnight

that's how powerful you are

you see a woman
near a lion
and you think
she needs to be saved
but if you look closer
you'd realize
that the lion
is her pet

———————————

stay away from men
who are bruised
by your womanhood

stay away from men
who'd rather explain
their lies
instead of apologizing

stay away from men
who wish to keep you small
while exaggerating their greatness

stay away from men
who believe you need them
despite the destruction
they've brought into your life

———————————————

it is never your job
to make someone deserve you

while you wait
for something real
be something real
and give you
to yourself

their opinions
of you
are not facts
that define
your worth

The day I realized that breaking you the way
you hurt me would not heal my heart was a
moment of clarity, true salvation.

A woman who realizes that she deserves
more is only dangerous to all the people who
wish her to settle.

We've been at this for a while now, me, trying to get you to remember your smile and all the things that filled you with joy before the madness entered your life. Can you fully recall the story of you, the girl who, despite her struggles, grew into a woman with a heart ready for war? Searching for peace of mind, someone to cherish, a love that didn't hurt. One day you meet a person, and you believe for one moment that they will be the one thing that travels consistently by your side into the future, only to discover that their true intentions were never mentioned, their lies disguised as truth. It hurts, and that pain remains with you for what you think will be a lifetime until you find your way out on the other side of a miserable space. You're here now, and I'm present with you. I know that feeling, maybe not exactly in the same ways as yours, but the pain and anguish are all the same. The uncertainty and confusion occur just before those moments of clarity. I offer my presence to you, not in hopes of saving you from anything or anyone. I just want to be here beside you when you win. I want to witness your realization of victory. I want a seat at the table when you decide to celebrate yourself because nothing will make me happier than to see you discover the joy that awaits you when you've decided to leave behind the people who intended to tear you down.

most of the men you meet
will be prisons searching
for strong women to hold
and no matter how strong
those bars
or that urge to give up

you must always keep fighting
to free yourself because you do not
deserve to be locked away

it's beautiful
the way you drink
the wild air
like sunflowers
beneath the sun
on top, a mountain

I started saving my energy for things that brought me joy. I had been yelling, screaming at times, hoping you'd hear the anguish in my voice, but the moment went unchanged, the disaster of you and I continued until I realized that I should offer you my silence and my absence because for once, you no longer deserved the distress in my voice, and the tension in my presence was never enough to deliver us from this hell. I went into the dark quietly in search of a light that eventually I discovered inside myself. And I don't even hate you; revenge was never actually the plan. Deep down beneath the wounds and the scars made by loving you, I hope you're okay, doing as well as I am. And even though you gave me nothing, I hope you made something out of yourself.

in this life
you will lose things
you will lose people
hell, you'll even
lose your fucking mind
from time to time
but in those losses
you will find yourself
and this is when you
will realize that winning
often disguises itself
as a loss

do not injure yourself
to save those
who rejoice
when you're broken

the heart is both
soft as rose petals
and tough, as brick

I had not intended to make it this far. I stood on the steps of us, afraid to walk down and away from the home we built. Moving on would be difficult but staying would be the pit of hell. And so I walked for miles with no real destination, just an understanding that there had to be some distance placed between you and I. There were days when I wanted to run back to you, but I knew life was not meant to be lived in reverse and the future would never place itself behind me. There were days when it hurt so bad that my heart began to blister, but the pain from loving you was all the motivation I needed to push myself further from that space of misery. And here I am, once plagued with the fear of emptiness. I discovered that I alone am all I need in order to feel whole.

Maybe the part of me I left behind was the
part of me that wanted to stay with you.
Perhaps that part of me had to be lost so that
I could find the fullness in who I've become.

Do not tame those ideas of wanting more.
Real love is a wild belief; be secure in your
understanding that you will never settle.

you will never
find the things
you need most
in the person
who tries to justify
giving you less

first, you feared the fire
then you learned
you could cultivate it
hold it like water
in a bowl
and so while others
see the fire and run
you see the flames
as an inspiration
to grow stronger

the silence between us
hurt more
than the silence
of being on my own

this is why I left

reborn
are those
who leave
relationships
filled with confusion

---

your troubles
may be stacked
as high as mountains
but you alone
are the highest revelation
of strength and what it truly means
to conquer what stands to stop you

no one is needier
than the man
who chases women
for sport . . .

Don't you think it's weird that the men who say you're insecure are also the ones who seek security in women? Or how they call you needy but spend most of their days chasing women they'll never actually deserve? You have boys parading as men, attempting to weigh down women who are much stronger than they are—asking you to settle for less because they are incapable of being more or doing enough to truly prove that they deserve your attention. How are you the crazy one when the man you're dealing with tells you that they don't want to be in a relationship but expects you to be completely committed to them? How crazy is that! It's time to start looking at this shit for what it really is, and it's time for you to start choosing yourself. It is never too late to leave a man who isn't a loss and has nothing to give you but a headache and regret.

you're single
you're dancing alone
moving to a song
that only you can hear
and I think that's beautiful

I don't know where you are in your journey, and maybe by the time you read this message, I'm just hoping you're somewhere safe. Somewhere closer to where you need to be to feel comforted by peace. I'm well aware that a clean break is not always possible, but even then, I still believe in your ability to put the past behind you and inch closer to your dreams. You've gone through hell and survived; you struggled through disappointment and regret, arriving here to this day, a bit wiser than before and stronger than you previously believed yourself to be.

I hope this message meets you in the middle of the night when you're restless or when the sun cracks open the sky, and you fight to raise yourself from bed. I hope these words remind you that though the battle is tough, you've already won because you have refused to give up on yourself.

I want you to know that I've been writing these messages because I hate the fact that people have become comfortable with doing all that they can to lose you. The ones who gain access to your heart should be the necessary things to keep you interested and hopeful in your pursuit of a love that lasts a lifetime. And I know it hasn't felt like it, but you are worthy. And I hope you find the strength to love yourself, adore yourself and appreciate the journey that brought you to this place and your body for holding up after being weighed down by sadness. I'm writing this to you because I care. I've always cared, and I always will. No matter the distance or time, I will always be here on the pages, telling you that you are more than they'll ever comprehend and that you are deserving of the most beautiful version of love.

She scares the hell out of men who want her to forget her ability to soar. So many have tried to ground her, and there have been times where they may have almost succeeded, but in the end, she flies high above all things and even higher than the people who do not deserve to be in the presence of an angel.

weary from holding on
wishing to be held
heart split in three
by shards of
broken promises

she's leaving in the morning
she's returning to herself

Family can be their own version of hell with a fire that burns so strong because you rarely see the chaos coming. When you're born into a tribe, you love those individuals by default; you trust them all the same, and so when their knives are pushed into your back, your heart feels like it's exploding from within. And the saddest part is that you become used to it after a while, so used to it that you begin to tolerate the evils in entertaining bad people for the sake of them being family. But it doesn't have to be this way. Not all breakups are of the romantic kind, and sometimes you have to find the courage to separate yourself from people you will be bonded to forever. There is a triumph in detaching from individuals who keep you from evolving emotionally. Some of the greatest stories of victory include breaking up with members of your family that wish to see you hurt and unhappy.

the moment
you think about leaving
a thing that no longer
makes you laugh
is the moment
you've won

the realization
that you can't
be happy
where you've been
is a victory
of the mind

and so, I hope
you go in the direction
of where
something better resides
I hope you fall in love
with yourself
this time

I began to listen to the silence; it took me a bit to understand that messages can be expressed at times without words. There is always something living within the emptiness and absence of communication. You've been there, too, trying to read between the lines that weren't visible. Struggling to comprehend everything that wasn't said. I sat there beside the person who had lost their desire to speak to me, and at that moment, I got the answer to all the questions I was too afraid to ask.

Don't be afraid to listen; that fear will keep you holding on to something or someone that has already left. Don't try to run from the silence; don't attempt to fill it with nonsense. Just listen to everything that isn't being said, and you will discover the truth.

we've reached the end
and it is beautiful
because of the possibilities
of starting over

I'm in awe of you
and I sit here
anticipating your arrival
to a place of peace
a place of joy
a temple, housing
all the things you deserve
a home built by you
with bricks made of
every experience you've had
good or bad

you're the fighter
that I'd bet my life on
you're the dream
realizing its own reality
you, a warrior
a survivor of things
refusing to cave
standing firm
on fractured ground
you are a movement
you are mighty
you are timeless